My Struggle My Truth

My Battle with Polymyositis

DIAMOND SAPPHIRE

To order additional copies of this book, contact:
Xlibris
844-714-8691
www.Xlibris.com
Orders@Xlibris.com

ISBN: Softcover   978-1-6641-7536-5
        Hardcover   978-1-6641-7537-2
        EBook   978-1-6641-7535-8

Print information available on the last page

Rev. date: 05/22/2021

ACKNOWLEDGEMENTS

I give thanks for God's Love. His Grace and Mercy. I thank Him for walking with me each and every day. Without Him I would not be here today.

I thank my beloved Mom and Dad for their support and love.

My strength came from my Dad. He's my hero. He was a quiet man with great strength. I saw that strength even when he was in pain. Dad taught me how to survive with whatever I have. Mom was there when I needed her the most. She was always caring and giving and became of her we never went without. I will be forever grateful for you both.

I thank my brothers and sister for the role they played in my life. I thank my children, who are my life. I thank them for their patience with a mom who didn't have it all together. I thank them for their love and support. I could not have asked for better children. I thank my extended family and friends who also provided their love and support.

I give special thanks to my cousin Tony Wingfield for the cover illustration.

LIFE GROWING UP

I am Diamond, and this is my story. One of my first childhood memories was growing up on the Northeast side of town. I grew up in a two parent household with my brothers, sister, and my Uncle, who lived with us for a short time. I remember the house vividly as it was a huge red brick house. It was the biggest house on the street. It was the first house on the street. When you walked up the stairs and entered the front door there was a hallway leading directly to the kitchen. On the left was a flight of stairs leading to all the bedrooms. To the right was the living room that we always called the front room. Straight back was the kitchen, pantry, and bathroom. To the right of the kitchen was the dining room and den area, where we spend majority of our time. Mom would not allow us to play in the front room. To the left of the kitchen was the basement. When you go into the basement there was a small room off the right. As you go further to the back it was open space. There was a room we called the coal room off to the right. We never stored coal there but it always smelled like coal. Now that I think about it. I think it was used for cremation. The upstairs had four bedrooms, bathroom and a "junk room" where mom stored everything.

My sister and I shared a room, and my brothers shared a room. We were told by people in the neighborhood that our house used to be a funeral home. We didn't seem too bothered by it. However, we did notice some strange things happening during that time.

For example, while playing in the basement sometimes we'd hear footsteps upstairs. Mom and Dad were at work so it couldn't have been them. So, we grabbed a baseball bat and creeped upstairs quietly and looked around. No one would be there, and we just laughed it off and went back to playing.

Dad said he saw the shadow of someone standing at the foot of his bed. Then it disappeared. My sister said she saw a man standing in the coal room. She went to get Mom and when they got to the coal room, he was gone. These type of situations made us believe that there could have been some truth to what people were saying. But what could we do? It was our home.

Across the street from our house was a gas station. I used to steal change out of mom's purse to buy soda, chips, and candy. Soda was only twelve cents. Mom kept her purse on a table in the hallway. I'd grab a handful of change when no one was looking to buy pop at the gas station. We lived near a busy street with a few small businesses. Next to our house was a Barbershop. I remember the owner of the shop being a man with green eyes. He was also a friend of my fathers. We called him green eye Jimmy whenever we spoke of him. His eyes were very light. Mom started that nickname. There was also a craft store where we bought paper dolls, stick on dolls, puzzles and games. I can't recall what the other stores were. They weren't important to me, I guess. We had fun growing up in the neighborhood. As kids we teased each other a lot. We didn't take what was said seriously.

We also went into abandon houses. We wanted to see what type of things people left behind. Sometimes we'd take things depending on what it was. We also played with other kids in the neighborhood. The neighborhood was decent with friendly people. I was called a tomboy because I loved hanging around my brother and his friends. My oldest brother was always serious and didn't joke much. He was either involved with the Boy Scouts or hanging out with friends. The times he was home we did have fun.

My sister and I played together a lot too. We loved playing with Barbie dolls, paper dolls, and misc items that Mom had around the house. Mom never knew we played with them. By the time she got home from work, everything was put back the way she had them.

I also have fond memories of my Uncle. How he used to drink a lot. He was constantly tripping and falling . My sister and I would hide and laughed at certain things he did. However, he mostly kept to himself. One time he cooked a rabbit and wanted us to taste it, but we didn't want to. He claimed it taste like chicken, but we had our doubts. Those were the last memories I have of him.

When I attended Elementary School, we were bullied a lot by a group of girls. I assumed they envied the way we dressed. Mom used to match our tops with our tights. Our outfits were never the same color. I'm sure people thought we were twins. We are only a year apart in age and we were about the same height. These same four girls used to follow us halfway home. They called us names and pushed us as we walked. We just kept walking. One girl even rubbed a booger on our back. We never said anything back to them or saw any of them alone. Although there were times we stood up for ourselves.

My brother had his share of bullying also. One time this boy chased him home from school. My brother got fed up and was tired of being bullied. He taught that boy a lesson.

My incident took place with a boy from my home room class. He had a crush on me but I didn't like him. He was always playing around as boys sometimes do, when they like a girl. He was very annoying. One day in class when I got up from my desk someone took my pencil. I automatically assumed it was him. He was always taking my things. He sat a few seats in front of me. I slowly walked over to his desk and popped him in the back of the head. I told him to give me my pencil. He had no ideal what I was talking about. He was however angry with me. He jumped out of his seat and chased me into the cloakroom. The cloakroom is where we hung our coats. There was no other place to run so we went at it. Everyone was standing around yelling. When the teacher came in, she made us return to our seats. After class he came up to me and swore, he didn't take my pencil. Maybe he didn't, I don't know. I just assumed he did.

My older brother had an incident outside of school. I don't know what took place. He came home with a shoe print on his back. Mom made a joke about it and said that someone must have been chasing him and when he fell they stepped on his back. She had us dying laughing. Mom always made jokes of our situation. We never knew exactly what happened. My brother never told us. Mom and dad never knew we were bullied or had to defend ourselves. They thought we were so innocent. Yea right.

Christmas was always a joyous time. Mom used to hide our presents in the basement under a pile of clothes. After searching we would always find them. We would be so excited to see what toys/dolls, coloring books, crayons, we got. We could hardly wait for Christmas. We also got clothes, candy, nuts and an orange. We absolutely loved moms holiday cooking, because she always cooked from scratch.

Dad was a workaholic but he was also a hands-on dad. He took us to the hardware store, the park, or Belle Isle. One particular day while spending time together at Belle Isle, I accidentally fell in the water. I fell where people go fishing. I was sitting on the edge with my feet hanging in the water. Dad was sitting in the car. I decided to bend over to touch the water. I tumbled over into the water head first. I vaguely remember doing a u turn and floated to the top. The water was a greenish yellow color. According to my siblings my arms were floating out to the side. I didn't say anything. In a panic they called to dad. Dad ran over and grabbed a big stick. He extended it out for me to reach. I grabbed the stick and he pulled me out. I spend the rest of the time sitting in the car in my underwear. I had to take off my clothes to dry them out. We did not leave Belle Isle until later. By then my clothes had dried out. Mom found out when we got home, she was furious.

Dad worked as a sanitation worker and Mom did domestic work. Dad cooked dinner most days because Mom either worked late or was out of town. However, there were times dad didn't want to be bothered with any of us. And we knew not to bother him. Dad loved sitting on the porch at night for hours. Sometimes he would sit on the side banister instead of a chair. The banister was made of brick and it was wide enough to sit on. That side of the porch always had a nice breeze coming throughout. Therefore I understood why he chose to sit there. When I looked outside, I would see him nodding off. I suggested he sit in a chair before he falls backwards. Of course, he continued to sit on the banister. By the time I went to check on him again the neighbor across the street was yelling, "Your father fell." Sure, enough Dad had fallen over the banister. He was getting up as I glanced over. He was okay other than a bruised head and ego. He decided to sit in a chair after that. I went inside to get the rubbing alcohol. As I headed back outside, I turned on the porch light so I could see better. He yelled, "Turn that light off," and I did.

At twelve, I baby sat for a lady who lived across the street. She was the one that told me Dad fell. She was really nice. She had four small kids. I didn't see the kids' father too often. I also helped to straighten things up at her house.

Also in reflecting back, there was guy who lived down the street. He was about four years older than me. I think he had a secret crush on me. He never said he liked me, but he always came around the house pretending to talk with Dad. He bought me my first record; Agent Double Ole Soul. I loved that song, and he knew it. Dad wasn't too crazy about him buying me a record.

I met my best friend K at Elementary School, in the fifth grade. We never had classes together. We started talking at the playground. She lived on the other side of Davison. We didn't visit one another at that time. We just talked at school. School was walking distance. This particular morning my sister and I left my brother behind. He was slowing around, and we didn't want to be late for class. Later someone came and got us out of class. We were told that there was an accident on the school grounds. That a semi truck had ran into the school yard. Our brother was one of the kids that were hit. So, they let us go home early. We walked home crying. We were afraid to walk pass where the accident took place. The fence was pushed in where the truck had ran into it. Mom and Dad were told later that my brother was pinned under the fence along with a few other kids. He had a broken leg and a few scratches. Other than that he was alright.

My sister and I didn't visit him at the hospital. Mom took pictures of him in the hospital. He seemed so sad. It seemed like he was in the hospital forever. We were glad when he came home, and he was glad to be home. We signed his cast. After some time, the cast started really itching. Dad gave him a hanger to use to scratch it. This only stopped the itching for a short period. Dad ended up cutting the cast off before it was due to come off. My brother never had any further problems with his leg.

Anyway we loved our house despite what people said about it. Some years later we eventually had to move. The City was building a freeway. The first few houses on our block had to be torn down to accommodate enough space for the freeway. We moved two streets over. It was a much smaller house. My uncle had long moved out by the time we moved. He later passed away due to an illness. I had just turned thirteen by the time we moved. I was still a daddy's girl. I used to hang out with Dad in the garage just watching him fix things.

When I wasn't hanging around Dad, my sister and I still did annoying things. For example we'd hide under this long buffet dresser mom had in the dining room. It was long enough for both of us to hide. We talked in a whisper. When we heard mom coming out of her room, we got quiet. When she passed us, we started laughing. She never knew we were under there. She would get so mad and yell at us, " stop that snickering. " As I got older Dad was the one who taught me how to cook. Which meant once I learned, I was always the one cooking. It was fun at first but became tiresome after a while. My sister did the house cleaning. She was really good at it. She told me Mom didn't like when it washed dishes because I never cleaned off the stove. We took turns washing dishes. I didn't think the stove was part of washing dishes.

Our quality time with Mom was when she tookus down south to visit my aunt. We rode with an older man and a female. He drove this huge old brown car. In looking back, I think it was a Cadillac. We enjoyed those trips. I liked visiting my aunt. We always had a joyous time. When we visited other relatives would always come by. I'd meet long distance cousins I never seen. As well as those I hadn't seen in a while. It was like a family reunion. Mom and my aunt cooked. Then every one sat around and talked about the good old days. I loved hearing about their life growing up. I felt at home. My cousin and I walked the neighborhood. It was very hilly in some areas. We went to the Underground where there were all kind of entertainment and food courts.

We also had a chance to see granddaddy. He lived a few hours away. We thought the world of him. Sometimes we stayed overnight with him and his wife. We didn't care too much for her. We just wanted to be with granddaddy. When he was around she was extremely nice. Granddaddy's first wife (my grandma) died at the age of forty-eight. We never knew her.

I loved the quietness of granddads place. Time away from the noise of a big city was great. No loud machinery, no one arguing over nothing, and no busy traffic. Even though I was young, I felt peace and solitude. I loved waking up to the smell of bacon or ham and fresh eggs and homemade biscuits. The sound of chickens chirping, cows mooing, pigs squealing and the roster crowing. I loved feeding the pigs, chickens and milking the cows. The only thing I didn't care too much for was the outdoor toilet (the out house). It was located a few distance from the house. When we took baths, granddaddy filled a huge wash tub with water and placed it on the back porch. It was a closed in porch. Granddaddy later build a bathroom onto the house. We took walks along the creek and threw rocks. We never wanted to leave when it was time to go. Those were the good old days.

Dad had a name he called us growing up. He called us Amazons, when we complained about our height. We hated being called Amazon. He said it meant strong warriors. In his mind it is a beautiful thing to be called Amazon. In our mind, it just meant we were big and tall and unattractive. My sister and I continued to share bedrooms. We had separate covers on the bed. My brothers had their own rooms upstairs. The upstairs was huge, actually It could have been a separate living area for a family.

My sister and I had a friend who lived down the street. We knew her since we lived a few streets over. Our dads were friends. There was times she wanted to play with us and there were times she didn't want to be bothered. Times she didn't want to play with us was when her other friends came around. She didn't have time for us then. So, one day while walking home from Middle School, my sister and I were talking and laughing with her. She said something that really annoyed me. I grabbed her by the arm and swung her around. She didn't cry but asked why did I do that. I didn't give her an answer. I'm not sure why I did it.

Come to think of it, I bullied another girl in the neighborhood. She was light complexion with long hair and quiet. I followed her around school saying things like, you think you're cute don't you, with your high yellow self. And other times, I just followed her not saying anything. But it all ended when her brother, who is much older than me came up to the school. He walked up to me as I walked down a flight of stairs. He told me to leave his sister along and slapped me across the face, then walked away. I cried as if I just got my butt whipped. Of course, I couldn't go to my parents because I was wrong. I would think that by my being bullied, that I would know what it felt like. I didn't bother or speak to her after that. Years later she and my sister became friends.

As my sister and I grew older our interest in things changed. She was always the neat one and I just didn't care how things looked. So, whenever we got into a disagreement, I would make matters worse by messing up her side of the room. What could she have done to my side, it was already a mess. She was so annoyed with me.

I recall one day my sister and I were in the dining room. We must have gotten into it about something. I started choking her while holding her against the wall. Mom heard the commotion from the kitchen. She walked in and yelled at me to stop choking her.

By Middle School I started hanging out with my friend K more often. We joined band together. We both played clarinet. I remember the music teacher who made me feel uncomfortable. My friend started coming over almost every day. She became part of the family. She ate dinner with us on a regular basis. Dad called her graceful. She never hesitated to jump on my brothers back. My older brother would shove her off and walk away. My other brother threw her to the floor and wrestled back with her. He didn't care. She didn't either. When it got late in the evening, we walked her home.

I started going to church with her. That was my first time at a Pentecostal church. It was a different experience. It was interesting. I enjoyed going. I enjoyed Wednesday night Bible study. I enjoyed the praise team. I soon joined the choir: The JBs. Since my friend and I were in the marching band in High School. We were asked by the Choir Director to play with the JB concert. I played alto saxophone and she played tenor. We were nervous but excited. I guess we did okay. No one said otherwise. I also enjoyed the prayer sessions we used to have. One evening I truly felt God's presence. We were at one of the Sisters house. We had been tarrying and praying. And as we were leaving to go home. I began speaking in tongues and could not stop. I didn't want to stop. I felt great. Afterwards, I thought to myself, *so this is the Holy Ghost.*

I eventually got tired of sharing rooms with my sister and decided I would move in the basement. I wanted to be alone. I wanted my own space. I wanted to listen to music as loud as I wanted. Some of my favorite artists were The Temptations,The Spinner's, The O'Jays, Elton John, The Chi-Lites, and The Average White Boys. I was also into jazz music. My sister and I still slept in the same room at night, so we were never totally away from one another. We just had different interests. I needed a place to getaway. I'm sure she did too. In my room in the basement, I painted the walls red and hung posters up. I had a loveseat couch. My sister and I did become a little closer after that. There was less arguing.

My First Boyfriend

I met my first boyfriend, Lucus at age sixteen. He was a friend of my brothers. The first time I saw him he was standing outside talking with my brother. My sister and I were looking at him through the living room window. We thought he was so cute. We thought he looked like a young Eddie Kendricks from the Temptation when he smiled. We got tired of looking at him through the window and started sitting on the porch. When he did come over, he and my brother would never sit on the porch. They either stay on the sidewalk or street curb because they just returned from riding their bikes. My sister and I decided that whoever he started talking to, the other one would back off, that was if he was even interested in either of us.

One day while sitting on the porch steps alone Lucus walked over to me and started talking. I was nervous as hell but played it cool. Of course, my sister was upset with me when she found out. I didn't care, I was now with the guy I had been secretly stalking. He and I started hanging out. In High School everyone knew we were a couple.

By this time my friend K had met my cousin and we started doing things together, the four of us. We went to the movies, the park, out to eat, the State Fair and so forth. I will never forget the time at River Rouge Lucus and I got into an argument and I wanted to go home. Since my cousin and K rode with us and wasn't ready to leave, he wasn't either. I was so angry with him. I snatched the keys out of the ignition and threw them as far as I could. They searched for the keys. I refused to. The times I acted like that Lucus never said anything. I have to say he's a good person, especially having to put up with me.

Lucus and I spend a lot of quality time alone. We sat in the basement on the couch with the lights out many times. There was a small black and white TV down there. Dad would come home and yelled from upstairs. " turn em lights on." We would jump up and turn on the lights. We then look at one another with a stupid look on our face. When I became sexually active, I had no idea what I was doing. Mom never talked to me about the facts of life. I asked him what happens if I got pregnant. He suggested some type of foam product he'd heard of. I don't recall the name. All I know is that it came in a pink box and was very messy.

I ended up pregnant in 1972, the same year I was to graduate. I'm not sure how many months I was. I just noticed my clothes fitting tighter and throwing up after I ate. I guess it was a little noticeable with certain clothes I wore. Mom did not have a clue because I avoided her as much as possible. I do not recall doing a pregnancy test. I just had that feeling. I told him I was pregnant, and he asked if I told my parents and I said no, not yet. He then said, "Well you are beginning to show." I didn't know how to tell my mother. I hadn't even told my sister. I was just taking each day as it came.

One night Lucus decided to call Mom and tell her I was pregnant. Mom came in my room and woke me out of my sleep fussing. Of course, she also woke up my sister. After she finished fussing, she went back to her room. I got out of bed and went to her room. I didn't really say anything. I just stood there. She told me to go back to bed. I was so disappointed that Lucus didn't let me know that was his plan. I couldn't sleep after that. He and I hadn't even talked about what we wanted to do. And Mom never asked what I wanted to do. I felt that she was not supportive or even tried to understand what I was going through.

Arrangements were made for me to go down south to terminate the pregnancy. Abortion was not legal during this time. A family member knew someone who did abortions. Mom was quiet that next morning. I looked at her and said, you don't love me any more with tears in my eyes. She hugged me and told me she still loved me. Afterwards, I sat on the couch in silence. My sister sat next to me and asked if I was sure that's what I wanted to do. I continued looking down and nodded yes. But I wasn't sure. I had not thought about the what ifs. My concern at that time was my mother not loving me anymore. Dad never express his thoughts one way or another. He probably knew it was a matter of time with us being in the basement in the dark.

My brother could not understand why I got to go to out of town and no one else could. I don't know what reason Mom and Dad gave him. A few days later Dad and I flew South. We didn't say too much on the plane other than the basics. Once we arrived, we spend a few hours at my aunt's house. We later drove to some ladies house. She was pleasant. She inserted some sort of instrument in me and that was it. A short time later we drove back to my aunt's house. She suggested that I get in bed and rest. She then gave me something to help relax me.

I recall other relatives came by to see us. They were glad to see Dad. My aunt told them I had whiplash from flying and did not feel too well. I dozed off and woke up feeling nauseated and weak as if I was drifting away. Then I felt like I had to have a bowel movement. So, I forced myself up and went to the bathroom. That's when I aborted the baby, just that quick. I felt too weak to get up, so I sat on the toilet to gather up enough strength. My aunt probably figured something was going on because I was in the bathroom too long. She came in to check on me. She helped me up from the toilet. I hadn't even flushed the toilet because I was too weak. She asked if I saw what it was, and I told her I didn't look. I never asked my aunt if she knew the sex of the baby until recently. My aunt say she doesn't know. I am not sure if that's the truth or not. Maybe it's best I don't know. I felt even closer to my aunt after that.

A few days later Dad and I flew back home. Of course, Lucus came by to check on me. But I didn't have too much to say to him. I was still angry with him for taking it upon himself to call *my* mother. I started being cold towards him. I wanted him to feel some of the pain I felt. I probably would have carried the pregnancy full term if I was given a choice. This changed our relationship. I kept telling myself I hated him, even though I didn't. We continued to see one another but things were different between us.

We did however went to the prom together. At least I thought we did. However, after talking with my friend K, it seems we were a no show. I have no recollection of ever being there myself. I do remember mom taking pictures before we left home. I wore a long mint colored dress with a long coat that matched. Lucus had on black pants with a mint-colored suit jacket. I also vaguely remember us driving to the prom. For some reason there was alcohol in the car. Maybe to party afterwards. I don't know. But what I do know is that I took it upon myself to open the bottle and started taking sips. I remember laying on his lap while he drove. And that's all I remember.

I was always quiet in High School. I didn't start speaking my mind until well-in my twenties. And people would take what was said the wrong way. I'm not sure if it was the tone in which I said it or the words I used. I was constantly apologizing for something I said. That is until it became annoying. So I stop apologizing. However my message was received, so be it. I'm saying this to say that it was out of character for me to drink like that. I wanted to open up and have fun that night.

K and my cousin arrived to the prom late. My friend said she asked different people if they seen me. After being at the Prom a short time, my cousin took her to a hotel. She said she asked, why were they going to a hotel. He told her that's where the after party was taking place. She said they walked into this huge room where people were partying. She asked Lucus where was I and he directed her to a bedroom. She walked into the bedroom to find me laid across the bed, knocked out. She asked what was wrong with me. She was told I had been drinking and had not eaten. That I threw up. She and my cousin left soon after. K said she kept calling to see if I made it home okay. I didn't get home until the next day. My mind is a blank in regard to everything that took place that night. Neither Lucus or I ever talked about that night.

K and I worked a few jobs together. One job was at a fast food restaurant. We had fun working together. We snuck food and hid in the basement to eat it. One of the supervisors had a crush on her and the other one had a crush on me, which meant we got away with a lot of stuff. They even invited us to their place for a so-called party. When we got to the house, it was just the two of them. We stayed and talked awhile then left.

We also worked at a nursing home together, donut shops, doctors office, etc. We may not have worked a particular job at the same time but followed one another at some point.

K and I even lived together once. It was a flat above her grandmother. Lucus and I were often not in a good place. It was mainly because of my attitude and I did whatever I wanted to do. He was never aggressive with me. I truly have to say he was a kindhearted person and a hard worker. He had a decent job. I was always moody and angry for no particular reason. Reflecting back, he tried me one day. He thought he would take my radio because I asked him to leave. He made it as far as the back stairs. I jumped on his back and started fighting him. He never hit me back. He just tried to restrain me or block my hits. We scuffled a minute and I got my radio.

The next day K's grandma said she heard us scuffling. I thought the flat was nice, except for certain things. One of them was that K's uncle kept trying to talk to me. He lived downstairs with K's grandma. I told K and she told her grandma, but what could she really do with him. He was grown. The bathroom had a low ceiling, and it was slanted. It reminded me of an attic. I didn't care too much for the bathroom. This is what affected me the most, the mice. Oh my God! I did not sit in the living room because of them. I stayed out most of the day and spend majority of time in my room when I was home. One day I looked behind the radiator and there were a lot of dead baby mice. That was the last draw. I was never comfortable in my own home. K's grandma set traps but it wasn't enough. I ended up moving back home. K stayed there a little longer. My sister was no longer at home. She had joined the service. I had the bedroom to myself.

After returning home K and I was trying to figure out what we wanted to do, as far as as some type of career. Her mother told us about this school for Lab Technician. It was a two-year curriculum at an Academy. Majority of the students were women. We signed up for the course and buckled down for the next two years. There I met two other friends who are twins. I got pregnant the following year. When my son was born it was a few months before I graduate. I ask a friend down the street if she would babysit for a couple of months. She was nice enough to do it for me. I appreciated that.

RELATIONSHIPS

I met my oldest son Trubbs father, at a wedding I attended with a couple of other friends. Who are sisters that lived on the East side of town. He was in the wedding party. He was standing at the back of the church lining up to walk down the isle. As I walked in, I happened to glance in his direction and our eyes met. He had the sexiest big brown eyes. Even though he wore glasses I was still able to see his eyes. At that time, he was seeing someone and so was I. Since my friends knew him, I ran into him periodically. They attend the same church. We ended up exchanging numbers and started hanging out. It soon became serious. He broke up with his girlfriend, however not because of me. I was seeing Lucus off and on, so that was not an issue. He later introduced me to his family. His sister and I became close.

K and I sort of drifted into different directions. We still kept in touch. We just didn't do everything together as we once did. I started going to church with the sisters who lived on the east side. That gave me the opportunity to see Trubbs father more often. That is whenever he came to church. However, the Pentecostal church I first attended was still my church home. He and I ended up in a committed relationship. After a year or so I became pregnant. He was the one that told me I was pregnant. I knew it wasn't Lucus because we were not in an intimate relationship. I was about seven months pregnant when I saw Lucus again. Lucus and I did start hanging out again but only as friends. I even offered to paint his kitchen cabinets while pregnant. I got extremely tired after painting and we cuddled on the couch for a while. Then I left and went home.

When Trubbs was born his father wasn't there for his birth. However, Lucus was. I remember that day all too well. I was home washing dishes and began feeling mild pains in my stomach. Mom and Dad took me to the hospital. Since I had not dilated much, I was sent home. So, mom and the neighbor across the street decided to go shopping. Within an hour the pain got worse. So, I told Dad that I think it's time to go back to the hospital. So, he took me back to the hospital. After I was examined, they checked me in. Once I was settled in the room Dad came in looking a little worried. He said, "I don't know why she decides to go shopping knowing you could have this baby." I can tell Dad was nervous and really did not want to be in that position. I assured him I would be okay, and that he could leave. I gave him the rings I had on to give to Mom. He asked if I was sure that I would be alright. I said yes, just let Mom know they kept me.

By this time, it was around six in the evening. I didn't know Lucus had come to the hospital with Mom. They were in the waiting room until almost eleven o'clock. No one had told them I had the baby. They didn't ask until they were worried that it was taking to long. Lucus visited me the next day. But never mentioned he was there the evening before. I'm not really sure what he was thinking or feeling. He gave me a card and on the inside of the card he wrote 'enjoy your life with your new son.' I knew our friendship had come to an end. I was hurt but didn't say anything. After that I would see him at church, and we spoke in passing. It was always an awkward moment for me when I ran into him.

After graduating from the Academy I got a job at a Hospital as a phlebotomist. I work the newborn ward. I hated to draw blood from those babies little fingers or heels. I wasn't sure if that was something permanent I wanted to do. I later enrolled in a community college, part time. Taking one or two classes at a time. I only took classes I liked, fun classes. If the class wasn't what I thought it was, I dropped it. I didn't know what curriculum to take. I was still working at the hospital until I no longer wanted to draw blood from babies.

I left the hospital and got a job at the Postal Service working midnights. By this time, I had my own place. Trubbs was about two-year-old. I had no one to watch him during the day when I tried to sleep. So, I could never fully sleep. Every sound would wake me up to see what he was doing. There were times Trubbs's father watched him.

I was so tired and sleepy at work. I'd take quick naps on my lunch break. I also took NoDoz to try and stay awake and function on the job. But the NoDoz made me feel nauseated. I always felt like crap. I was exhausted. I eventually quit the Postal Service which was a good paying job. I was young and stupid. He and I began to have problems with the relationship. A few years later we decided to go in different directions.

After I quit the Postal Service I went back to working as a Lab Technician for a private doctor. Shortly after K also got a job at the same place. I was still in school part time. When I needed a babysitter, K recommended someone from church. I met with the person. She was a very nice person but didn't say much. She had children of her own. They were able to help watch Trubbs. This person also lived closed to my job, which was very convenient. I also received food stamps and funds to pay for a babysitter, which helped out a great deal.

After a few years I left that job and started working at two other doctor's office. Each job was no more than two days a week.

I eventually moved on to other relationships. Casual dating here and there, some were serious. My sister and I usually met guys at house parties or through someone we knew. One guy I met at a house party was more interested in my sister. I secretly had a crush on him. He and my sister went out on a date. When she was getting ready to go out with him, she assured me it was nothing serious. However I quickly got over it.

I guess I was trying to find myself with so many different relationships. I've had good encounters and some not so good. I will only discuss a few relationships out of many. This particular relationship did not turn out well. I was involved with a married man.

However, I did not know he was married. I met him in one of my classes. We eventually ended up dating. He'd take me to his house, but it was always at night. I didn't see anything that would let me know he was married or that a female lived there. Although I really wasn't looking for anything. He and I saw one another often. We took trips out of town with Trubbs. Trubbs was about five. This guy was always available when I called or wanted to do things with him. The times I didn't see him, he said he was on Reserve duty. He said he had to go out of town during those times.

One day his wife found my resume. He was supposed to have turned in my resume to one of his doctors. His wife called and told me that they were married. First she questioned me as to who I was. His wife was calm as if that was something he did on a regular basis. Of course, I didn't believe her. She said if I didn't believe her, to call his mother. I called his mother after receiving the number from his wife. His mother confirmed that it was true. His wife worked the night shift which explains why I was only allowed to go over his house at night. Also you can't really see the house that well at night. I was so upset with him. He almost caused me to have a nervous breakdown. That's how serious the relationship had become to me. It had a profound affect on me because he had asked to marry me. He even gave me an engagement ring. I called his wife back to apologize. She and I decided to set him up. I was to meet at their house. She was to call him at work and ask him to come home.

He lived about an hour away. Once again, being young and naive I went to meet up with him and his wife. It was dark out but I didn't care. I was furious and did not think about what could have happened to me. As I stepped onto the porch, the lights inside instantly went out. I knocked on the door anyway. I could hear the dog barking, but no one came to the door. I knocked a few more times then left. His wife later told me that he would not let her come to the door. When I finally was able to reach him. He said he didn't open the door because he didn't want to face the both of us at the same time. He admitted to being married but claimed they were in the process of a divorce. I think she would have mentioned that, unless it was something he wanted, and she didn't. I ended the relationship. I went to Mom and cried. I told her what happened. She tried to console me. I gave her the engagement ring because I no longer wanted them. She said she would put them up for me in case I wanted them back later.

Another short-lived relationship was with a guy I met while working at a doctor's office. At first, I didn't give him the time of day. He really wasn't my type. He kept pressuring me, so I gave him my number. The relationship was one sided. He was looking for someone to basically take care of him. After staying over night a few times he didn't want to leave. He got very comfortable coming and going. I finally told him he had to leave. That was something he did not want to hear. He got so angry with me. I guess he figured if he had to leave, he was going to punch me in the face. When he punched me, I fell to the floor. It happened so quick that it took me a minute to realize what happened. By the time I got myself together, he was leaving out the front door. I crawled over to the door and pushed it shut. Trubbs was coming into the living room as I was getting off the floor. He didn't say anything and neither did I. I don't know if he witnessed what took place or not.

After that incident that guy had the nerve to come by the house when I wasn't home. I knew it was him. The front door was made of wood and there was a crack in it. I assumed he was knocking really hard or kicked the door. Dad asked what happened to the door. I told him I didn't know. I did not want my family involved in crazy decisions I made. I didn't see him any more after that day. He never returned back to work.

I have been hit by two other men in my life. Once by Dad because I made a smart remark to them. I had never said anything smart to him before. I don't know what possessed me to do it this particular day. My sister always talked back and got away with it. When I did it, I got back handed across the forehead. He had on a ring which left a mark above my eye. Mom was furious and told him he could have put my eye out.

The other person that hit me was another family member over a parking space. There was limited parking in front of Mom's house. This family member lived upstairs at the time but I didn't. I assumed it was where they normally parked. I told them they didn't own that spot. We were standing inside the back doorway which lead to upstairs. We were arguing back and forth. All of a sudden I remember falling back against the stairs. I had to go to the emergency room. I had to have stitches put in.

One other causal dating was with a guy who I will call Damon. He was extremely nice. Every time we went out to dinner, he always invited my mother. Damon was a little too nice. I later found out why. He used to park two or three cars on the side of my house. It was a vacant lot next to me. He said he fixed cars for people. I thought there was no harm in doing that. I allowed him to park cars there. I just let him know that I did not want a lot of cars parked there. Dad had passed away by this time. Dad never would have allowed it. One day a police officer knocked on my door inquiring about the cars. I told the officer what I knew. I was told by the officer that the cars were stolen. My heart dropped. The officer said there would probably be a court hearing. He ask if I would testify in court. I did not want to be involved in that. Damon asked me not to testify. But the police officer threatened that my children could be taken away since I have knowledge of what was going on. I was not having my children taken away. So, I went to court. I have never been so nervous in my life. Damon kept looking at me in court as if to intimidate me. I never saw or heard from him after that.

Another relationship was with a friend of my other brother. My brother didn't care too much for our dating. He never gave a reason why. His friend who I will call Steven, came over one day looking for him. He wasn't home. So, Steven and I sat on the couch in the living room and talked for about two hours. We seemed to have a lot in common. I had a son, and he had a daughter about the same age. He came by another time. When I told him my brother wasn't home, he said he didn't come to see him. We talked again for hours then started hanging out together. Steven told me he was married but was in the process of a divorce. Maybe that's the reason my brother didn't approve. Steven always bought little gifts such jewelry, candy, or cards. Once he bought me a winter coat. We dated a few years then the relationship ended. I cannot recall the reason, but I do know it was not on bad terms. I ran into him again after my incident. He was in the store with his daughter. I think I never felt totally comfortable with him in the relationship. I felt intimated by him. 1 couldn't be myself. I'm not sure why. He was never physically or verbally abusive. We only talked a few minutes then exchanged numbers. I visited him at his apartment. Nothing sexual happened. We just caught each other up on what was going on in our lives. Communication stopped after that. I ran into Steven again years later while working at a Hospital. He tried talking to me again. This time it felt as if he wanted to be more than friends. I lied and told him I was in a relationship.

I met my second oldest son Smokeys father in Canada. Four of us, my sister, myself and two other friends took a girl's trip to Toronto. We each met someone except for one of the friends. We had a fantastic time dancing and partying. We exchanged numbers. After that trip we went back to Toronto a few more times. Smokeys father and his friend visited us a few times. After Smokey was born he saw him a few times. When he sent clothes for Smokey they were too small and looked like girl clothes. Therefore, he was never able to wear them. A long-distance relationship became too hard to maintain. So, the relationship eventually ended. He didn't see Smokey after the relationship ended but continued to send gifts on his birthday. But that also ended after some time.

I met my daughter Lelas, father while attending a data processing class. I was on my way to the Lady's room, and he spoke to me. He kept asking me questions. It caught me off guard. I got close to the wall and slid my shoulders along the wall as I walked. I don't know why. I was a little shy. It was not an immediate attraction to him but yet I felt uneasy. However, not in a bad way. He and I started dating. We were married seven months later. He had two children and I had two. Smokey was about a year old. His two kids lived with us for a short period but ended up moving back to his mothers because of minor problems we were having.

When I got pregnant with my daughter, He could not understand why I was constantly sick. I laid around quite a bit but still did what I had to do. We lived next door to Mom and Dad but eventually moved about a few miles away. We slowly started having more problems. Majority of the time he went to bed first. He always had the TV blasting all hours of the night. We both had to get up for work. He could sleep with the TV on, I couldn't. When I asked if he would turn down the volume, he claimed he couldn't hear it. I got tired of dealing with it and moved my things into my daughters room. He kept asking me to come back in the room, but I wouldn't. We had other disagreements as well.

Another incident was one day while taking a bath he knocked on the door because Lela was crying. He acted like he didn't know what to do. He asked what should he do, and I didn't answer. After asking me a few more times with no response, he forced the door open. "I said, that's supposed to make a difference because you force the door open?" He just turned around and left. We never sat down and talked about our problems. I didn't give it all that I could have. There were other things going on in our relationship. I chose not to deal with it. I wanted to be married and at the same time, I didn't. I felt trapped. I decided to make plans to move back next door to Mom and Dad. It was ridiculous to live in a situation I wasn't content with. I was able to move back because Dad owned the house. One day while my husband was at work Dad and my brother moved out all of my things. Dad had a big dump truck. When my husband got home all of my things were gone. He called asking why did I leave. I had mixed emotions. I sort of wanted to go back. But I was not going to put my family through moving my things again. I didn't move back in with him. He came over often to see Lela, but we never got back together. We divorced when she was about two years old but remained friends. I just wasn't ready.

After I had my daughter I tried to get my tubes tied. I knew I didn't need any more children. I didn't try to get them tied following her birth as I should have. It was a few years later. My sister-in-law took me to have the procedure done. I was awakened in recovery only to find out that the procedure wasn't done. I felt like I went through surgery. I felt awful. I was told by the doctor that they could not perform the procedure. The reason the doctor gave was they were not able to put me to sleep. And I'm thinking, *put me to sleep. You woke me up, was I not asleep*? I was so disappointed and hurt to find out nothing had been done. My sister-in-law took me to Mom's house. I crawled into her bed and closed my eyes. My sister-in-law felt what I was going through. She got sick and had to lay down also. I teased her about it later.

I met Baby boys father, through a friend D. I visited her at work one day. He saw me in passing. D said he found me attractive and wanted my number. At first, I didn't want her to give him my number. He was cute but a little shorter than what I preferred. He continued asking about me, so I finally told her to give him my number. The relationship was like any other relationship with it's ups and down. We were together about three years. However, it seems like when I got pregnant with Baby boy is when things got worse and remained that way. I'm not sure if he wanted that responsibility of raising a child. He never verbalized it but his action proved otherwise. We drifted apart. He wasn't there for the birth of his child. My sister took me to the hospital. Prior to having baby boy I made sure arrangements were made to have my tubes tied. So my tubes were tied and burnt before I left the hospital. Baby boys father saw him a few times after that. At first he didn't really believe Baby boy was his child. He requested a DNA test, which I was more than willing to do.

RAISING CHILDREN

Raising children was a struggle as well as a blessing. I almost burned down the house one day when Lela was a baby. She had wakened up crying for her middle of the night feeding. I got up and put a pot of water on the stove and placed the bottle of milk in the pot. I was tired and decided I would lay down while the bottle warmed up. I woke up to a house filled with smog. I quickly jumped out of bed. I ran into the kitchen and snatched the pot off the isle. I then turned the stove off and opened the doors to let the smoke out. I checked on my kids to see if they were still breathing. The thought of what could have happened hunted me for some time. The next day I talked to my friend K and told her what happened. She then proceeded to tell me, she was awakened from her sleep with me heavily on her mind. She said she just started praying. I know that was God.

I truly enjoyed the times I spend with my children. They were brought up in church. I think church is what kept us grounded. Trubbs is the only one who is still committed to going to church. I also did spare of the moment things with my kids such as painting cartoon characters on the wall. Characters like as Mickey Mouse and Goofy. I even painted a gigantic robot on the wall in their bedroom. I can't remember the name of the robot. I know my children thought I was a little crazy sometimes. I even painted Mom's entire house in two days.

My children always played well with one another. They spent majority of their time playing outside. When they were inside they occupied their time playing games like Simon said, Pick up Sticks, Slinky, Game Boy, GI Joe dolls, Barbie dolls, Connect Four, Uno or Nintendo. Nowadays kids are given too many choices. Sometimes the parents have to be the wiser and choose what's best for their child. Today kids do not want to do anything else but play Videos Games and iPads. Too much Videos games or iPad is not good. They don't know how to do anything else. You tell them to go outside and play, they will look at you as if you were crazy. They do not know what it is to read a book or use their imagination for fun things to do.

My children constantly used their imagination. One day they build a fort out of blankets while I was at work. The fort extended from the front room into the dining room. When I got home I was pissed, to say the least. I made them take it down and clean up their mess. But they enjoyed things such as this. One thing I did not tolerate was letting my children stay overnight at other peoples house. They could however have their friends come over. I was just comfortable knowing where they were and what they were doing.

My children loved it when their grandparents' barbecue. Every one was outside together with the music playing and the smell of barbecue. They also took that time to ride their bikes. Trubbs had his bike stolen one day when he rode to a fast food restaurant. The person who took his bike was someone from the neighborhood. Someone driving by saw what happened and gave him a ride home. My sister was in town around that time. She sat on the porch hoping to see the person who took his bike.

I will never forget when I took them to the park one day. Trubbs decided he wanted to take his LEGO set. I told him to leave it in the car but of course he did not. He chose to carry this tub of LEGOs with him to the park. When we got ready to leave the park, he dropped the container on the ground. All the LEGOs scattered everywhere. I was so angry with him and made him leave them on the ground. He cried begging me to let him pick them up. I was tired and ready to go. I told him that he should have left them at home like I told him. I also said now some other child has a LEGO set. Trubbs will bring that up today. I guess he never forgot either.

I wasn't always a stern mom. There were countless times we had fun together. We joked, acted silly, made things together. On Halloween I made their costumes. Sometimes I bought mask or made up their face. At Easter we'd dye eggs and sometimes hide them. We went to church Easter Sundays and they always had new outfits. Thanksgiving and Christmas dinner were spend at moms house. She always cooked. My children rarely ate fast foods. When they did, it was a treat.

I allowed my children to have a pet at some point. They had a goldfish which someone fed oatmeal to and it died. My daughter had gerbils. One of them got out and I could not relax until it was found. I freaked out. They found it that same day behind a chair. To me, they look like mice, and I'm terrified of mice. My daughter ended up getting rid of them when the mother bit the babies head off. I was glad to see them go. As my daughter got older, she also had a rabbit. She named her Sapphire. When Sapphire died, my daughter was crushed. It hurt me to see her so upset. They buried Sapphire in the back yard. It took her some time to get over it.

Baby boy had a dog he named Diamond. He got her as a puppy. She was an American bulldog mixed with Lab. She stayed in the house as a puppy. He had to keep her outside when she got bigger. Diamond was a good dog. Baby boy didn't take care of her like he should have. And even though Mom didn't really care that much for dogs, she fed Diamond every chance she got. I guess she felt sorry for Diamond. Baby boy and Trubbs ended up taking Diamond to the dog pound. Baby boy didn't have time to walk or take care of Diamond. I was a little sad to see her go.

At first, I struggled with having four children with different fathers and having to rely on the system. Then I thought, whoever has a problem with my children having different fathers that's their problem. As far as being in the system, I also worked. Also, in some cases women who have four children with the same father are in worse situations. The fact that they have different fathers did not make things better or worse. I love my children, and no one walked in my shoes. My parents were the only ones who were totally supportive. Raising four children was not an easy task.

However, my children were well mannered. When I took them to restaurants people complemented me on how well behaved they were. My children knew I did not play. They can act out at home but not in public. My children were given chores to do. I believe that if I had not given them chores, they would not have become responsible independent adults. Children need structure. My children showed me no disrespect. When I'm out sometimes I see children having temper tantrums and the parents not being able to handle them.

My children were mischievous sometimes, such as running the babysitter away. I don't know what was said but the babysitter told me she was not be able to watch them any more. When I asked them about it later, they still wouldn't tell me what happened. They just laughed. I remember another time when I had new windows installed, one of the guys showed an interest in me. We exchanged numbers and I invited him over one evening. When he came over and as soon as I opened the door, Baby boy and Lela burst out laughing. He was a lot older than me. I made them go to their room. I still heard them laughing which meant, so did he. I was so embarrassed. After that evening I never saw or heard from him again.

When you have children there is always that possibility that one may not like you. Smokey and I never had that bond when he was born. I was going through postpartum depression. I always felt sick and had migraines for two weeks from the epidural I received. When he cried, I changed his diapers, fed him and laid him back down. I wouldn't cuddle him or talk to him. And it seemed as if he cried all the time. The neighbor across the street said she could hear him crying. As a baby he threw coffee mugs at me. He wasn't even walking yet. He was in a walker. Growing up I never treated him any different from my other kids.

As a teenager he waited until I was in bed and asked for something. When I tell him no, he stood by the side of my bed or in the doorway and asked why not a hundred times. Many times he would eventually walk away if I ignored him. Although there were other times he didn't. Trubbs heard him and told him to come out of my room. And he did with no problem. Maybe he thought things should go his way. That I'm not supposed to use the word 'no' with him. He got so annoying that I put a gate at the kitchen entrance to keep him from coming in my room. Both him and Trubbs bedrooms were upstairs. They still had total access to the kitchen. They didn't have a shower upstairs. They could only take baths. So once a week I'd open the gate to let Smokey take a shower. And he took a shower and went right back upstairs. For the most part I did not lock the gate during the day.

I recall one day driving home from grocery shopping, Smokey started going on and on about something we discussed. After trying to explain what I was saying, he answered with the most outrageous examples trying to make a point. But his examples would have nothing to do with what we were talking about. I became so annoyed. I had a bad headache. So I asked him to stop talking. He continued to talk. I threatened to put him out the car if he didn't be quiet. He continued to run his mouth. I pulled over and told him to get out and he did. At that point we were a mile and a half from home. I didn't even look back. I just drove off.

Trubbs began to worry about him when he thought he should have been home. He was on his way to go and look for him when Smokey walked in the house. He did not say anything or look in my direction. He just headed straight upstairs. He got along great with his brothers and sister. However, when he got older, we had a closer relationship. He made oldies CDs for me. And I took him grocery shopping or to Kmart and pay for his items. Our relationship went in a different direction when I offered to pay his security deposit on an apartment. I guess I didn't get the money to him quick enough. So he sent me an email saying, I told him I was going to pay his security deposit. And that I should not say it, if I wasn't going to do it. I read the email and went off on him. I told him I was doing him a favor, that I didn't have to pay for anything. I then told him how ungrateful he was. But not in a nice way. That's when he stopped talking to me. When I ran into him at the mall, he'd speak after I spoke first. He was always cordial.

Trubbs was a good-hearted child. Always trying to make someone happy. He was always protective of me and his siblings. He and I wrestled all the time. However, that doesn't mean he was always innocent. One day I sent him in the store to buy diapers for Baby boy while I sat in the car. I wondered why it took him so long to come out the store. When he finally came out, he was escorted by security. I was told that he had taken a video. He was given a strong talking to and put on punishment.

However, Trubbs and I have always had a close relationship. He's my go to person. It's always easy talking to him. He can come to me as well if something was on his mind. Sure, there's disagreement as with any mother and child. He would get into his moods, but they never last long. As he got older, he didn't have the best work history. I told him if I am able to go to work every day, so could he. I ended up moving out the house leaving him and Smokey. Smokey was seventeen and he was twenty-two.

My relationship with my daughter was a world wind. As a child she was a sweet happy go lucky person. It was during her teenage years we started to bump heads. She was constantly in her moods for no apparent reason. We could be having a decent conversation and it would be something I said that she didn't like. Her mood automatically changed like a light switch being turned on and off. When she was in a good mood, we got along great. She moved out and moved in with her dad as soon as she turned eighteen. She and I have a good relationship. She still doesn't let me know certain things going on in her life. She is a very private person.

Baby boy and I did not have that fun time of doing things together as I did with the rest of them. He was about three when I came down with my illness. He was always quiet. I believe he felt cheated. I'd tried talking to him, but he would not talk to me. He would sit on the side of his bed as if he didn't hear me. When his siblings teased him about something, he'd directed it toward me. When he came home from school, dinner was always cooked. He'd come out his room, fix a plate and return to his room. Numerous times I'd try to have a conversation with him, and he wouldn't say anything.

I'm not sure of what was really on his mind. He didn't invite me to his games and would later say "You didn't come to my game." How could I, if I never knew when they were. He got upset with me for speaking with his coach about his weight loss. He had lost so much weight within a short period of time. I was concerned about him. He also got annoyed with me when he pulled his shoulder out of socket. He had to sit out a game, per my request. He had a difficult time expressing his feelings. I could see the hurt and pain in him. I didn't know how to reach him. I did not know how to get him to open up. His relationship with Lela was not in a good place during this time. It was just him, Lela and I living together.

When Baby boy was seventeen, I tried to talk to him again to let him know I was considering moving. The house was becoming too much for me to keep up. Lela had moved out. Baby boy half cut the grass or shoveled the snow. I never had a problem with him doing whatever I asked him to do. But he was not always home when I got off work. The times he wasn't home I sat in the van until he came home. That was only when I felt nervous, thinking it was too much ice or snow on the ground. I eventually let him know I found an apartment. I told him to let me know what he wanted to do. He had the option of moving with me or staying at the house until I sold it. I said I would help with the bills.

I needed to know before I put the house up for sale. Baby boy never did let me know. I continued trying for a few months then finally put the house up for sale. When I sold the house, he had about a month to move out. He later apologized for not responding and said he now understands what I was trying to do for him. Today, he and I have a good relationship. Baby boy has my back as well. My children all have their different personalities which makes them unique. I may not always like them, but I love them for who they are.

I realize that my illness had a profound affect on my children. It affected me as well. I missed out on doing so much with them. I often felt guilty for not being able to do things with them. I couldn't go certain places with them because some places wasn't wheelchair accessible. All things considered I'm truly blessed. As a single parent my children turned out great. Things could have easily turned out differently. They all competed High School. Trubbs now works in Technical support. Smokey resides in another state. I'm not sure what his job consist of. Lela has a PhD and Baby boy is a Chef. And I have so many beautiful grandchildren.

Death of My Father

Dad passed away in 1987 on Valentines Day at the age of sixty four. I was about four months pregnant with Baby boy. My dad has always been my rock. I had the notion he would live forever. This is how I saw him. He was the strong silent type. Certain people called him the friendly giant. If something bothered him, he rarely let it be known. But if he had something to say, he would definitely let it be known. He was always there for his family. We were never without. I don't recall being afraid of anything when he was around. He taught me so much. How to cook and fix things his way. By that I mean what ever he fixed may not looked the best, but it worked. If he was in the garage working on something, I was right there. He also loved his grandchildren. He taught Trubbs so much. Smokey wasn't the type that cared to learn how to fix things. Dad also enjoyed his one on one time with Lela. He sometimes kept her while I worked.

It hurts me to see that he didn't get to enjoy his retirement. He was a diabetic and loved sweets. He also had high blood pressure. One he cut himself while clipping his toe nails. After that he constantly had problems with his foot. It did not heal. He tried home remedies. He refused to go to a foot doctor. I could see the pain in his face. It got so bad that his toes look like they were burnt. He had to use a cane to assist with walking because of the pain. Dad did not want people to see him walking with a cane. He was a proud man. I was finally able to convince him to see a doctor. When I took him to the foot doctor, he was given a cream to put on his toes. His blood pressure was so high that the floor around the toilet was sticky after he used it. On a few occasions he passed out because his levels were so high. Yet he still refused to see a doctor.

The last time I heard Daddy's voice was when he woke me up one morning. He wanted Trubbs to help shovel snow. We lived next door at that time. Usually when I'm awaken from my sleep, I would have an attitude. This particular day I didn't. I just said okay. I woke up Trubbs and told him his granddaddy needed him. He was about twelve. He got up, got dressed and went out to help. Shortly afterwards, I heard Trubbs banging on the door. He was yelling. I knew something was not right. I walked swiftly to the door and opened it. He yelled, "granddaddy fell." I threw on a coat and went outside only to see Dad lying on the cold ground face-up. His eyes were open, but they looked glazed. Trubbs later told me that he turned Dad over because his face was in the snow. I sat on the ground next to him and laid my head on his chest. I could hear him breathing but it was different. It was a harsh shallow sound. I'm not sure who called the ambulance. Mom came out of the house and called his name. I said, "stop mm,he can't hear you." I don't know why I said that to her.

When the ambulance arrived, I told Dad I love him and got up. After the ambulance left, I got dressed and called a friend to stay with my kids. I called my sister. I kept saying, daddy's dead. She told me to stop saying that. I knew he was already gone because my brother had already called from the hospital and told me. He'd already picked up mom and taken her to the hospital.

I drove to the hospital after my friend arrived. Dad was lying in a room with a sheet pulled up to his shoulders. He looked so peaceful as if he was asleep. He had an expression as if he was getting ready to smile. I leaned over and kissed him on the forehead. At that precise moment I felt a sharp pain in my stomach that only last a few seconds. And in my heart, I felt it was Dad's spirit. Baby boy does have an old soul. So does the soul of a person pass on? No one knows for sure. Baby boy loves old cars, and music, that's before his time. The kind of music I didn't think he would have an interest in. He has Dad's strong quiet spirit. He's a family man like Dad was.

I recall the day after dad passed. I was sitting next to the vent in the dining room trying to get warm. My sister came up to me and said she dreamed that Dad was caught between two worlds. I wasn't sure what that meant. I suggested we pray. We held hands and just prayed for some time. The following morning when I went into Dad's room it was shining so bright as if the sun was right there in his room. I couldn't believe what I was seeing. I called mom to come see how bright his room was. I told her about the dream and how we prayed. She said he probably wasn't ready to leave us. She said he's at peace now.

Dad you weren't one for words, but I know you loved us.
You were my strength through dark times.
You we're always grounded and strong.
You were like a tree that couldn't be moved.
However one day that tree became weak from the elements of life and fell.
And even though you're no longer with me. You will always be my rock.
Miss you so much Dad.

Prayers like this one keeps me going.

2 Corinthians 4:17-18

For our light and momentary troubles are achieving for us an eternal glory that far outweighs them all. So we fix our eyes not on what is seen, but on what is unseen, since what is seen is temporary, but what is unseen is eternal.

The Holy Bible-new International Version

Events Leading to My Diagnosis

Well, let's get to the problem at hand. I was working early shift as a phlebotomist at the Hospital. I remembered having a cold that I could not get rid of. I had that cold for over a month. It was continuous coughing and sniffing. My body ached in certain areas, especially my thighs and just above the elbows. I simply attributed the pain and soreness to my having worked out. I had a workbench at home where I did arm and leg lifts. Afterward, I would be a little sore. My coworker commented that the pain and soreness were due to my thighs trying to support my big butt, which I did have. Of course, we just laughed it off. Shortly before this time I had a hepatitis B shot. Health Care Worker were required to have a Hepatitis shot if they were going to be exposed to blood on the job. *Could this have been the cause of my problems?* I don't know. Anyway, it was a gradual onset of three to five months. Toward the end of December, I became extremely tired and fatigued. I forced myself out of bed every morning, not wanting to take my kids to school but knowing I had to. I sat on the side of the bed a few minutes before I could actually gather up enough strength to stand up. Some mornings I actually cried because I felt so tired and exhausted. It was as if every ounce of energy was drained from my body. However, I forced myself to do what I had to. After all, I did have four young children depending on me, the youngest being two. Once I was up, I felt somewhat better, but not much. So, I dropped them off at school and then headed to work or to class. During this time I continued working two part-time jobs while attending community college. I guess that's a reason to be exhausted.

I also recall one day while driving home, and as I attempted to make a right turn, I was not able to make that turn, not without force anyway. I had to really grip the wheel with both hands and forcefully turn the wheel. Naturally, this frightened me. This was just the first incident. When I got home from a long day and tried to climb the stairs to my porch, I had to stop midway and rest a minute before I could continue up the stairs. Now while all this was going on, mind you, I was going back and forth to the doctor, trying to find out what the heck was going on.

I was given a prescription for multivitamins, and one doctor had the nerve to prescribe muscle relaxers. That was a joke since I was already experiencing muscle weakness. I didn't take them. Various tests were done, and the results kept coming back negative. I have always considered myself a strong, independent person who was in good health. I exercised regularly and took vitamins. However, it turned out I was wrong on both accounts. I did have to depend on someone and, as it turned out, was not so healthy either. Although, I do believe that daily stresses in my life—such as the loss of my father, divorce, working two part-time jobs, attending school, trying to be that perfect mom, played a significant part in the breakdown of my immune system.

What really scared me was one day while singing in the choir at church, my eyes started bothering me. I thought to myself, *these lights are extremely bright tonight*. Finally, I could no longer take the bright lights and left the choir stand. I went to the bathroom and put water on my eyes hoping it would help. I felt somewhat better, so I decided to sit at the back of the church, where there was less light. My eyes continued to bother me, and it became difficult for me to focus. A church member said my eyes looked glossy. I kept blinking, trying to get my eyes right. After a few minutes, I decided maybe I should just leave. I had to pick the kids up from my ex-husband's house. I remembered saying to myself, hurry and get home. Something just didn't feel right. I finally made it to my ex-husband's house. I would normally stay a minute and chat with him and his wife, but not that day. I didn't mention what was going on to them. I just got the kids and left.

As I drove home, my vision became worse. I could barely see the car lights in front of me. I kept riding my brakes, thinking I was getting too close to the car in front of me. Then I picked up speed, trying to get home as quick as possible. I kept squinting my eyes from time to time in order to see the traffic lights, which appeared blurry. All along praying that God would get me and my children home safely. It seemed to take hours for me to get home, when I was actually only two miles away. I made it home by the Grace of God. I put the key in the lock, opened the door, and threw everything on the floor. I kept saying I can't see. Trubbs started to get a little worried.

I decided to call my best friends mother. Her mother and I always had a great relationship. She was also a nurse at one time. She suggested that I put a cold or warm cloth on my eyes. I can't remember which. Then she suggested I lay down for a while. She said if it didn't get better to call her back. Well, I ended up calling her back. As soon as I hung up from her, I lost my sight. I called to Trubbs to dial the number and informed her of what happened. She sent her daughter Stacy to take me to emergency.

When I got to ER, I was asked the usual questions and taken to the back immediately. Some kind of drops were placed in both my eyes. I eventually fell asleep. I woke up when I heard my friend K's voice. I still wasn't able to see until sometime later before leaving the hospital. I was told that I had some sort of infection. I went home thinking, *oh my God. What's* going on. I immediately went back to the doctor for more testing.

It got to the point where my gait became unsteady, which caused me to walk a little wobbly. My speech became slurred at times. I could no longer raise my arms above my shoulders. I recall K and I joking about it one day. She had come by and I was in the kitchen. I grabbed a gallon of milk out the refrigerator. I told her I couldn't sit the milk on the top of the refrigerator. I tried but couldn't. I looked at her and we both laughed. I was also losing weight, but my appetite remained the same. When someone grabbed my arm, it was tender. It became more difficult for me to get up from low places, such as the toilet, bathtub, and couch. However, I was still driving, even though I probably shouldn't have been.

I was still working, dreading each day, each moment. One of the doctors I worked for became very concerned. He asked if he could run an HIV test, free of charge. I guess he thought maybe I had AIDS due to my symptoms and unsteady gait. I agreed to have the test done, which came back negative. My illness was a mystery to everyone. It was thought that maybe I had multiple sclerosis (MS). That was understandable, with symptoms of muscle weakness, blurred vision, loss of coordination, etc. My symptoms were very similar to MS. I was even willing to accept that I had MS. At least then I would have a name to my illness. I was just tired of being tired.

Diagnosis/Hospitalization

I went back to the medical doctor for him to review my lab results. He informed me that there was definitely something going on. My enzyme levels were steady going up, especially my CK (creatine kinase) level. My primary physician suggested that I have a muscle biopsy to try and determine what was going on, if possible. I had the muscle biopsy. They removed tissue from my thigh. The results finally came back and I was called back into the office. My doctor informed me that I have Polymyositis. "Poly what?" Was my response. I had never heard of such a disease. I was diagnosed in 1990.

'Polymyositis is an autoimmune disease, which are disorders of the immune system where the cells that are responsible for identifying and destroying harmful invaders mistakenly identify elements of the body's own tissue as foreign and attack it. The immune system can distinguish between substances in the body that belong there and those that don't. The immune system attacks a foreign or abnormal presence in your body but is then supposed to stop the attack before damaging the body itself.'

My immune system had become weakened for whatever reason and started attacking my muscles, thinking it was a foreign substance. The cause was unknown. I was told that it could have been a virus, but the doctor didn't know for sure.

According to the Mayo Clinic, 'Polymyositis Is an inflammatory disease that cause muscle weakness affecting both sides of the body. This condition can make it difficult to climb stairs, rise from a seated position, lift objects or reach overhead.'

"Polymyositis most commonly affects adults in their 30s, 40s or 50s. It's more common in blacks than whites, and women are affected more often than men. Signs and symptoms usually develop gradually over weeks or months. There is no cure for polymyositis; however, treatment and therapy can improve your muscle strength and function. The muscle weakness associated with Polymyositis involves the muscles closes to the trunk, such as those in the hips, thighs, shoulders, upper arms and neck. It affects both sides of the body and tends to gradually worsen. The exact cause is unclear, but the disease shares many characteristics with autoimmune disorders, in which your immune system mistakenly attacks your own body tissues."

When I was diagnosed my world instantly turned upside down. It was a hard pill to swallow. I questioned why. There were no answers. I felt that it was no way out of the situation. My children has always been my life, my main focus. To be a single parent sucked. I was no longer in control. However, I knew I couldn't just give up. I had to continue fighting. To try and over come this huge obstacle that was affecting my life, my family.

Since I was diagnosed, I've only met three other people diagnosed with Polymyositis. This is how rare it is. Shortly after the muscle biopsy, I was hospitalized because my symptoms became worse. It was around February of 1991. I was thirty-five years old. Even though I had a good appetite, I Lost 70 pounds within a three-month period. I only weighed 114 pounds at five feet, ten inches tall. My normal weight was between 170 and 190.

The weight loss didn't seem to be that much of an issue to me, but to others, it was. I just thought my clothes were fitting a little better. By the time I was hospitalized my CK level had shot up to 1200. I was immediately started on ninety milligrams of prednisone intravenously and weekly methotrexate. While hospitalized, I could no longer walk, turn over in bed, or speak clearly. According to my family, I was hallucinating and didn't recognize anyone. I didn't even recognize my own daughter when she came to visit. My daughter was seven during this time. I was told that I just stared at her, not saying a word. This had to hurt her, wondering why her mom didn't say anything to her.

When one of my other friends visited, I called her K when she attempted to feed me. Someone had brought balloons and hung them by the window. I thought the balloons were the devil. I thought my brother was my deceased father. I'm not certain as to how long I had been hallucinating. When I finally started coming around, I had to relearn how to add, subtract, and recall certain things. I exhibited short- and long-term memory problems. I had slow recall and dysphagia, which is difficulty in swallowing and respiratory problems. It's weird because during this whole ordeal, in reflecting back, I don't recall being sad, depressed or afraid. Actually, I didn't recall having any feelings at all. I was just basically there, according to my mother. I remember the Pastor came by the hospital to pray for me. When he entered my room. I was sitting on the toilet chair behind the curtain. I told him I was unable to meet with him and why. I'm not sure which one of us was more embarrassed. He left and I didn't see him again. Not at the hospital anyway. He prayed for me later at K's sister house. I was hospitalized for about a month and a half.

However, I did become afraid and worried when one of the nurses told me that when I go to rehab, I would really have a hard time. The nurse told me that the staff at the rehab facility were going to work me extremely hard. I felt that was something she could have kept to herself. I assumed her reason for making such a statement was because I wanted to return to bed shortly after I was up in the Geri chair. However, there was a legitimate reason for my wanting to go back to bed. The Geri chair was extremely hard on my tailbone. I was in constant pain. Don't forget, I only weighed 114 pounds. Sometimes it would hurt so bad that I felt like crying. I was not able to shift my body to relieve the pain because of weakness in my shoulders and hips. I could never reposition myself when I needed to. When I called for the nurse to put me back in bed, of course no one came. I knew they heard me calling out. I heard them talking amongst themselves at the nurse's station. I continued to call out, and the next thing I heard was someone calling my name. At the same time calling for backup assistance. I could not see them or respond. I heard one nurses say, "She's having a seizure," as they lifted me back onto the bed. I've never had a seizure in my life prior to that. I was later told that I had over a hundred seizures while hospitalized—unbelievable.

Rehabilitation

I was eventually transferred to rehab. I was terrified thinking about what the nurse had said. As staff rolled me out of the elevator on a stretcher, I noticed the dreadful-looking blue walls. It wasn't bright like the hospital. It felt as if I was on a prison ward or in a basement. I was put in a room with three other women. I was not able to reach the phone to let my mother know I was transferred to rehab. And I didn't know if anyone notified her that I was being transferred. I kept thinking that she'd be wondering what happened to me. I couldn't relax from worrying. I wanted so badly to call to let her know. I called for the nurse. In all honesty, no one had come to check on me since I arrived. As usual, no one claimed to hear me calling out. I'm panicking now. I continued to call out once again. The next thing I know, I was back at the hospital.

I was later told that I had another seizure and that a code blue was called on me. The hospital notified my family, and they were told to get to the hospital right away. According to my friend, I had died for approximately six minutes. My sister lived in another state. She was told that I had passed, so naturally, she was very upset. I'm not certain how long I was hospitalized that time. When it was time to return to rehab, of course, I didn't want to go. I talked to a hospital social worker and explained my situation. The social worker was very nice. She assured me that everything would be fine and that nurse should not have made that statement. I assumed the social worker gave staff at rehab the heads-up, because when I returned to rehab, I was put in a bright-colored room with only one roommate. Everyone was pleasant and tentative.

The only thing I had a problem with was mealtime. We were not allowed to eat in our room unless we weren't feeling well. I had to eat in the dining area with people with disabilities. They required some form of adapter to assist them with eating. It was so depressing to be in a room with so many people facing various challenges. I didn't feel that I fit in the same category as the rest of them, when actually I *was* in the same category. I even used a device to assist me with lifting my hand to my mouth.

I was still not able to walk, stand, turn over in bed, or go to the bathroom without assistance. I absolutely hated taking showers because the bathroom was always cold. I had physical therapy and occupational therapy every day to help strengthen me. To help me learn how to adapt to a new way of life. I was eventually allowed to receive visits from family and friends.

Prior to being hospitalized, I was involved in a relationship with someone. Since I was not able to walk or give him a definite answer as to whether I would ever be able to walk again, he walked out of my life. He only visited once. I was devastated and felt so alone. It was a time I needed him the most. It takes a tragedy like this to show who people really are. I didn't have answers to give him as far as when or if I would ever be able to walk. The doctors didn't know what improvements I should expect, if any. I went through rehab angry and rebellious. Angry for being in the situation and rebellious because I figured, what was the use in trying. I just wanted to sulk and wallow in my own pity.

I began feeling better when I met a special young man. He was a quadriplegic and very carefree. He had a great personality and a sense of humor. He didn't seem bitter about what happened to him. He was ten years younger than me. He always had a positive outlook on life despite his misfortune. He was truly an inspiration. I looked at his situation and asked myself what reason do I have to be depressed. He motivated me to move forward with my life. I started listening to gospel music every day. It also became my inspiration. When it was finally time to be discharged from rehab, the doctor wanted to discharge me to a nursing home because my children had chicken pox. So, I lied and told the doctor that they would not be staying in the same household.

RETURN HOME

When I went home, I kept in touch with the guy from rehab. We talked on the phone for hours. He just lifted my spirit so much. When he was discharged from rehab, I visited him at his apartment. My brother dropped me off and picked me up. At that time I used a manual wheelchair to get around.

I didn't start walking again until shortly after I returned home. Watching my mom run around caring for me and my children didn't make me feel good at all. I could see that it was taking a toll on her. Some days she seemed exhausted. She had her hands full I admit. So, one day, sitting on the toilet chair, I wanted to see if I could stand on my own. So, I decided I would try no matter what. I was able to stand on my own with a little effort. I was so shocked and overcome with joy but didn't say anything to mom. My hospital bed was a few feet away. I decided to take a step to see if I could walk over to the bed. I was able to walk over and sit on the side of the bed. I was truly proud of myself. This time I called to mom. She was in the kitchen preparing dinner. Mom was so amazed and happy for me.

After my follow-up doctor's appointment, I started going to outpatient rehab, using different transportation companies to take me. I despised riding in those vans. In some of the vans I sat so tall that I had to lean forward all the way to the rehab facility and back. One day, I wasn't strapped in properly. When the driver pulled off, my wheelchair went straight backward. I hit my head on the floor quite hard. I was so annoyed with the driver. He was worried and kept apologizing and asking if I was alright. I didn't bother to report the incident. Luckily I wasn't hurt.

Another time, I was going to an appointment along with Lela and Baby boy. This time (a different driver) the driver ran out of gas on the freeway. He pulled over to the side and walked to a gas station, leaving us along in the van. I was sitting in the front seat, complaining about him running out of gas. It took what seemed like forever for him to return. I was bored and tired of waiting. The driver had a pack of cigarettes sitting on the seat. I told Lela and Baby boy I should take one of his cigarettes and smoke it. Yeah, I know, bad influence. Anyway, I took one and lit it. I held it while watching it burn, then threw it out the window. I don't even smoke. I did it for the heck of it. Rehab eventually ended, and I was able to walk up and down steps. I used a cane for short distances.

Some time had passed with my walking using a cane. I then wanted to see if I could drive. I got in my car, which was parked on the side of the house. I drove down the alley to see if I could work the gas peddle and brakes. Once I knew I could manage that, I drove around the block. I was so proud of myself, thinking there was hope yet. I didn't really start driving until I was able to prove to rehab that I could. So, I was sent to one of rehab's driving evaluation class to be tested. I passed the test without needing any driving device.

Coping with a New Way of Life

Years later, I'm still using a cane for short distances, and a scooter chair for long distances. I am no longer able to climb stairs. I'm still not able to reach above my shoulders, or get up from a low sitting position. I have a strap to lift my legs in order to put on pants. I have a shoehorn, which I added an extension handle, to be able to put on my shoes. It's still difficult to turn over in bed or to even get in and out of bed. To lay down, I sit on the side of the bed, lay on my side, then use my leg strap to lift the right leg into the bed. I then brace my right foot against the foot board or wall then lift the other leg. Once that's completed, I scoot my back side over toward the center. This way I won't fall out of the bed when I turn on my side. Even scooting is difficult because I'm not able to lift my butt. I have a rail on the side of the bed to help maneuver myself.

It's another struggle when I get up in the morning. I turn on my side, scoot back a little so I won't be too close to the edge. I raise the head of the bed, swing one leg around at a time. I then hold onto the grab bar while feeling for my shoes on the floor. Once my shoes are on, I reach for a strap that I have lined along the bed, then pull myself to a sitting position. I then sat on the side of the bed for a few seconds then stand up.

When I get dressed, undressed, or do my hair, I leaned on the dresser or shelve in order to reach my hair or pull a shirt over my head. Doing my hair is truly a hassle. So, I would either wear braids or wigs for the most part. I also have what's called a reacher to pick up things. However, if I tried to pick up something too heavy, the reacher was useless. I also have a raised toilet chair and different things to make life a little easier. I don't sit on the couch or regular chairs. I normally sit in a high-back-office chair, which becomes uncomfortable if sitting too long. I did have a lift chair until It seemed as if I was about to fall forward when standing. The lift chair leans you forward instead of straight upward. It is still a challenge and sometimes frustrating to do certain things.

When I'm eating or drinking I use my left hand to brace my right arm then lift my fork or glass to my mouth. Usually, people don't notice because it's not that noticeable.

When I get up from a sitting position, I spread my legs slightly apart to support myself with standing. My children always hated the way I stood up. They always tell me to place my feet closer together then stand. That never works for me because my legs feel weaker when I do it that way. My outer thighs seem stronger.

I am able to get up from the toilet and office chair on my own. I have a tub bench for showers. My daughter helps with showering. I now also need help with getting up from the scooter chair or out of the van. I used to be able to get up from my scooter and out the van on my own. I blame my decline in those area on the parking attendant at my old apartment. I parked at the front entrance of the building to be closer because usually I walked in. And the parking attendant parked my van for me. When I get out the van, I'm slow so, the attendant would say, " Come on here" and preceded to help me get out. She wasn't mean or anything, she was actually very nice. I assumed I was keeping her from parking other cars. Which was understandable. After that I started asking for help from the attendants rather than try on my own. When someone rushes me, I tend to move slower.

In the beginning of my diagnosis, I was able to go up and down stairs. But I would be very tired and a little weak once I reached the top step. Sometimes I get to the top step but not be able to push up on my leg for that last step. One time Lela and I stayed with my sister to help her following surgery. She had a flight of stairs to the second level. I got stuck at the top step. I could not step up on the platform. Lela had to put a chair on the platform. I sat down on the chair and then stood up. I avoided going up stairs after that until I was done with everything for that day. Going downstairs was much easier.

It got to the point I could no longer do stairs at all. I can't even step up a curb without fear. The last time I tried going down the stairs was at work, during a fire drill. The office was on the eleventh floor. I made it down two flights of stairs and could not go any further. My coworkers had to get the emergency escape chair to take me down the rest of the way. The next day, my hip was in so much pain and continued to hurt for sometime afterwards.

I used to have a step-in shower. However, taking a shower in the walk-in shower one day I fell stepping out. Of course, I was home alone. I normally hang my cell phone in a plastic bag within reach outside the shower door. As I stepped out the shower, my right leg felt extremely weak. So, I stepped back in the shower and reached for my cell phone. When I did, I dropped the phone on the floor. So, I had no choice but to try and get out of the shower. As I thought would happen, while attempting to get out again, my leg gave out. I went down. Luckily for me, I was able to reach the phone I dropped. I called my husband and my daughter. It seemed as if it took them forever to get there. Once they got there, they place a chair in the bathroom. They both lifted me onto the chair and then helped me up from that position. Thank God I wasn't hurt, just cold and sore from lying on my side for twenty minutes. After that I only took showers when my husband was home.

Cooking wasn't a problem for me, unless I'm trying to put something heavy in the oven or get a heavy pot out the cabinets. I'm not able to bend forward, even slightly, or I would be on the floor. So, in order to put something in the oven, I braced myself near the counter and stove and then put food in the oven. This was done at an angle, not directly in front of stove. Once the food is cooked, I take it out the same way. Cooking on top of the stove was not a major problem. Except if I'm trying to cook something on the back burner. It's more convenient to leave dishes in the drainer after I washed them. Mom and I did grocery shopping together. I did my own laundry, using a reacher to take things out of the washing machine or dryer. I mopped the floor using a light weight mop. I held onto the wall while mopping. I swept and used long handled dust pan. I was not able to vacuum.

I now understand that sometimes someone has to suffer in order to realize how blessed they really are. Since my diagnosis, I have accomplished a great deal. I raised four loving children and was able to return to school and still work.

After receiving an Associates Degree in General Studies, I went on to earning, a BSW, and an MSW. I decided to go back to school because I felt working as a Lab Tech was no longer feasible for me. It just wouldn't work. My experience with trying to get into college was not a good one. When I wrote my admissions letter, I explained my situation. I received a response back, asking if I had thought about going into social work realistically. The word *realistically* was in bold print and stood out at me. I responded to the letter, stating yes, I have thought about it realistically and this is what I wanted to do. Of course, after that I was accepted.

When I first attended College it was not wheelchair accessible my first semester. There was no ramp to get into the main building front entrance. I had to go through the back entrance with security. I had to do the same for the other building located on the grounds. The main building had stairs, so I had to make sure all my classes were on the first level. The second building had an elevator. When classes ended for the day, I had to locate security to take me back through the back. By second semester they had installed a ramp for both buildings and also a chair lift for the main building. Once everything came into play, I enjoyed attending classes. I was taken to and from college by a transportation company.

I once had an incident in class with my wheelchair. It was a pink motorized chair. I loved it. The key broke off when I turned it on. The teacher contacted maintenance department and they came up to my class and put a switch on my chair. This meant

I no longer needed a key. I was truly grateful. Maintenance later made me a lap table that folded over to the side when not in use. I felt special. I also made the schools newsletter. After receiving my Bachelors I attended a University. I thought I was big time, not allowing my disability to stop me. Getting to classes was much easier. I found employment while working on my Masters degree.

Work Experience and Disability

Since I was diagnosed, I had to endure so much discrimination. I not only had to deal with being a black female in the workforce. I now have to deal with being a black female with a disability. When I interviewed for my first job as social worker, the department Director questioned whether I could do the job. However, my supervisor saw something in me and was willing to give me the opportunity. And for that, I am forever grateful and often told her how much I appreciated the opportunity.

I worked as case manger doing outreach service. Which meant I worked at nursing homes and assisted living facilities. I worked extra hard to prove my self worth. The pay wasn't great, but it gave me a chance to get the experience I needed. I recall having to meet a client at court for a hearing. I was driving and using a scooter chair to get around. I had a van with a scooter lift. I always tried to arrive early wherever I go to allow myself time to get the scooter out. This particular day, I was glad I did. It was raining, and I was rushing trying to get the scooter out so I wouldn't get too wet. Once the scooter was out, I then attempted to unhook the strap to release the scooter. I stumbled over the back wheel and fell over the seat part of the scooter. The seat was folded downward. I wasn't able to get up. I called out for someone to help I soon heard a male's voice saying, "I'm coming."

He asked what he could do to help. I told him to stand behind me and lift under my arms and pull me to a standing position. He did and it worked out fine. He asked if I was okay, and I said yea and thanked him. By this time, I was soaked and a little shaken up. I called my supervisor once I got inside to inform her of what happened. My supervisor asked if I was okay. She said I could return to the office if I wanted to. I assured her that I was fine and went into court to meet with my client. Everything went well.

Other things have happened while at work as well, such as one day when I was crossing a busy street, my scooter just stopped right in the middle of the street. It was only for a few minutes. However terrifying minutes. I later found out that a news truck was parked across the street and the signals interfered with my scooter.

After working for this organization for six years, I put in my resignation. I was doing my internship at an hospital. They offered a stipend plus I always enjoyed working at hospitals. My supervisor, and I remained friends when I left.

Working at this particular hospital was rewarding and sad. I worked on the rehab/long term care unit. I covered the hospice unit when my co-worker went on vacation or called in. Majority of the patients were able to return home following rehab. However, there were those who were not able to return home for what ever reason. Or maybe they didn't show enough improvement to live on their own. So they had to transfer to long term care.

When I covered the hospice unit sometimes it became a little emotional. I met a lady who was angry because she was dying. In the beginning she wouldn't talk to me. When she did speak to me she'd give short answers to questions I asked. I didn't give up on her even when I was no longer covering the unit. I'd stop by just to say hello and asked if she needed anything. She slowly began to come around and open up to me. She talked about her life and how she worried about what her son would do without her. She only had one child and he was an adult. She felt he needed her. He visited regularly. She was in constant pain and had some really bad days. I knew she was just holding on for her son. So, when I covered the unit again and following weeks of her going through this I met with her son. I told him that she was so concerned with his welfare that she couldn't leave him. I suggested he let her know that he would be fine and it's okay to let go. He agreed and talked to his mother that afternoon. The following day she passed away peacefully. That touch my heart. I was in tears.

I enjoyed my job tremendously. Unfortunately, after four years of working there I was let go. I did not meet the licensers requirements within the required time frame. I was a limited licensed social worker.

As I mentioned, employers claim not to discriminate, but they do. I went on several interviews after I left the the hospital without a return call. I believe employers could not see beyond my disability. It was easy for them to say there was a more qualified candidate. I did finally get a job at a nursing home but left there after a short period. I ended up going back to my previous employment working as Intake Worker. I stayed there until I put in for early retirement in 2013. I put in for early retirement because it was becoming more difficult to get out of my van without assistance. The security officers where I was employed assisted me with getting out of the van every day. For that I'm very thankful. I also began to lose interest in what I did. I was no longer excited about going to work. I no longer felt as if I was making a difference.

FEAR OF FALLING

I continue to deal with everyday life struggles. One would be surprised at the things people take for granted. Sometimes I become annoyed when people think that I can do it all. People tend to forget that I have a disability. Which could be a good thing or a bad thing. For example, when I was working, I got up at six a.m. every morning. And depending on what type of day I had at work I may or may not cook. Sometimes I'd go to bed at 7:30 or 8:00 p.m. My kids or friends made comment such as, "You in bed already?" Yeeess, I'm tired. It was an effort for me to do anything, so naturally, I was tired. It's an effort to reach in the cabinet to get a glass, cup, plate, canned goods, or whatever. It's an effort to reach the knobs on the back of the stove or put something in or take something out of the oven, to mop, sweep, make the bed, or wash clothes. It's a struggle to get in and out of bed, get dressed. It is still a challenge. As I said, people tend to forget that I have a disability or the extent of my disability.

If I'm standing and someone attempts to hug me or slightly nudge me, it's a possibility I will fall. It was always that fear. I don't have good balance. So, I'm always on guard, standing close to a wall to brace myself, just in case. When I lived in my apartment I walked in using a cane. Getting on the elevators made me extremely nervous, especially if it was crowded. Sometimes I'd wait on the next elevator even though it may be a long wait. I rather wait instead of squeezing in between people, which makes me uncomfortable. I could easily trip over someone's feet or get bumped.

There was another time when I was married to my second husband. We were at an doctor appointment, and I had to use the restroom. There were only three stalls, neither one were wheelchair accessible. They were also very small. You could barely close the door. So, I left my scooter outside the door in the hall with my husband. I didn't have my cane with me. I walked in with no problem. I had to use the restroom with the door slightly open. Even with the door open, it was a tight squeeze. This made me anxious trying to hurry before someone came in. As I stood at the sink washing my hands, something came over me and I couldn't move. I couldn't take a step. I was frozen with fear of taking that next step. No one else was in the restroom. I called out to my husband. He had to come into the women's bathroom to walk me out. Now, when I'm alone in a public restroom, I feel uncomfortable and a little anxious because I don't know when it will happen again.

Another incident was at the dentist's office, I got up from the dentist's chair and walked over to my scooter. I accidentally kicked the back wheel of the scooter and fell forward. I didn't fall to the floor. Instead, I fell into a bending position. Thank God my knees didn't buckle. I called for assistant from the staff. They stood behind me and pulled me up to a standing position, after I explained what to do.

I also recall a time I lived next door to my parents and Baby boy and Lela lifted my legs at the same time to take off my shoes. It was my birthday and they bought me a pair of house shoes. They were so excited for me to put them on. I was standing up talking to mom, and was not paying attention to what they were doing. I hit the floor so hard and landed on my tailbone in a sitting position. I yelled out and rolled over on the floor. Trubbs was lying on the couch sleep. He jumped up and ran over to me. He tried to help me sit up. I was in so much pain and told him not to touch me. I thought I had broken my back. They called 911 and the emergency attendants helped me up into a chair. The pain had eased up so I didn't go to the hospital. Baby boy and Lela felt so bad. They thought they had ruined my birthday. I assured them that I was fine and gave them a hug.

There are times I get frustrated with my situation. I've only actually fallen a few times, thank God. One time, I was trying to open the shower door, and it was a little stuck. When I pulled harder on the handle, I sort of fell forward. I tried desperately to prevent myself from falling to the floor. My plan was to try and sit on the toilet seat near the shower. I was holding on to the grab bar outside the shower. I tried to swing myself onto the toilet chair. At the same time thinking, this is not going to work. I ended up sliding to the floor. I just reached in my pocket, got my cell phone and called my son. I hadn't gotten undressed yet. I was getting things ready. I always made it a habit to have my cell phone on me.

Another time my scooter was parked in the foyer near my door entrance. I attempted to stand from my scooter. My legs were too far apart when I tried to stand. I was not able to bring them together. So, I then tried to sit back down and ended up on the floor. I don't recall calling anyone. I think my husband was coming in right after I had fallen. I made sure my kids have a key to my place, for situations such as this. So, this is why I'm always anxious and nervous. Falling, or the thought of possibly falling is extremely scary. The possibility of hitting my head or breaking something is no joke. There were many other small incidents.

Marriage/Relocation

Well, I will now talk about my second marriage. I thought I met that special someone who was willing to accept my disability along with my mood swings. I will call him Marshal. I met Marshal through K. He used to give her organ lessons. I've known of him for some time. K mentioned that she has always wanted us to meet. We never met at that time. He has always had an interest in her. On our wedding day his eyes were fixated on K as she walked away. He didn't even notice me looking at him. I was sitting right next to him.

Anyway, he and I didn't meet until around 1999. We met at my place of employment. I was working at an adult day care center. He was interested in having his father attend day care program. I interviewed both of them. Unfortunately, his father was not an appropriate candidate. We talked a little after the interview and exchanged numbers. After several phone conversation I invited him to my twenty-fifth-class reunion. He agreed to go after checking his schedule. So, I purchased the tickets only to find out later that something had come up and he would not be able to go. I was annoyed and disappointed. I ended up taking my daughter with me. He did apologize but I wasn't trying to hear it.

He tried making it up to me by taking me out to dinner. We met at the restaurant, so he really didn't take me, per say. Dinner went well. We talked periodically afterwards. I did most of the calling. I eventually stopped calling. Then he called every blue moon, then the calls stop. After a few years of no call, I decided to delete his number. A year later out of the blue, he calls. He said he ran across my number and wondered if it was the same number. We started talking again. I asked if he could give me singing lessons. Of course, the singing lessons didn't last long at all. Marshal later shared with me about his previous relationship. He was engaged. She became ill and he took care of her. He also stated that he wasn't sure if he could or even wanted to put himself in that situation again. He also thought I was more dependent than I was. Once he saw that I was independent with driving, working and caring for myself, he felt differently.

One day I mentioned I was going to Frankenmuth and asked if he want to go with me. Of course, he said he have to check his schedule. I told him, it didn't make a difference to me rather he went or not, I was still going. The next day he said he was cleared to go. This was around 2008.

We went to Frankenmuth and had a fantastic time. We started talking on a regular basis. He'd come over and I'd cook occasionally. He didn't stay overnight often. I went with him to church where he played organ. I loved hearing him play, but I never told him that. We went to movies, out to dinner etc. He started calling me his wife. We weren't engaged or anything. We did however started ring shopping the following year. Although he hadn't officially asked me. It was however discussed at some point. We just decided to look at rings to check out different prices. I did see a ring I really liked. So, he put the ring on layaway. I helped with the down payment. I told him the rest of the payment was all on him. The ring was sort of expensive.

We discussed what type of wedding we wanted. Marshal wanted a big wedding with six grooms and bridesmaids. I didn't care about all that. I was satisfied with just a best man and maid of honor. We couldn't afford an extravagant wedding. We opened a joint account to start saving for the wedding. Within the next few weeks that money was gone. I closed the account and vow to never open another account with him.

Prior to our getting married I asked if he was financially able to take care of me. He said it wasn't a problem. We also discussed our living together. He said he didn't have that much stuff. I had no idea as to how much stuff he really had. I never had the chance to go inside his house due to a flight of stairs.

When I told my daughter I was getting married she just lost it. She asked why would I tell her that on her birthday. She said she doesn't know him. I said, I do, and that it's my life. After that, my daughter did not speak to me for three months. I'd text asking how she's doing. No response. So, I asked K if she would be my maid of honor. She was more than willing to be my maid of honor. However felt that my daughter should be the one to stand with me. K said she would definitely step up if things didn't work out between me and my daughter. I broke down crying and told her about Lela's reaction when I told her I was getting married. My friend of so many years had never heard or seen me cry. She asked if I wanted her to talk to Lela. She called Lela and found out that she was just as hurt as I was, but too stubborn to admit it. Lela slowly came around. We went dress shopping together and made plans for the wedding.

The wedding was small. It took place in 2010 at a church chapel with Lela by my side. Baby boy walked me into the chapel. The reception followed with about one hundred and twenty people. It was nice, small and simple. We didn't plan a honeymoon. We decided we would take one later. We were both exhausted and fell right to sleep that night. We spend the rest of the week moving his things into my apartment. I had two bedrooms. This is when I realize how much stuff he actually had. He had the second bedroom filled to capacity, including the hall closet and storage room. The storage room was located next to the apartment. He had even given things away prior to moving.

Everything was good at first but after months of him not putting a dent in straightening out that second bedroom, I began to feel overwhelmed. I couldn't even see the bed in that room, let along go in there without having to move something out the way. Marshal would always say, " I'm go do it." He never did. I'm not sure if it was my nagging or his procrastination that affected our marriage. He claimed I wasn't affectionate during the day. As far as a kiss every now and then or my not wanting to hold hands. He always wanted his back massage. I didn't mind doing it every now and then. I even tried to spice up the marriage. I printed out questionnaires that we could ask one another to initiate conversation. I found different board games we could play together. I even signed us up for a marriage retreat. The retreat was really nice. K and her husband, also went with us. These things worked for a short time. Marshal then started staying up late watching TV in the living room. I suggested at least cuddle sometimes. When he did cuddled it seems he was always restless. I'm like what the hell. After a while I stopped trying.

I continued to ask when he was going to straighten up that bedroom. I asked what if mom needed to stay over again. She had stay once before either because her apartment was fumigated or it was the time, she had her appendix removed. I can't fully recall. Promises, promises were all I would hear. I informed him that he had access to the entire apartment which wasn't fair and, that I was limited. So, I finally suggested that he sleep in that spare room until he gets it together, hoping that would motivate him. It didn't, not really. He started sleeping in the other room, even though he wasn't too happy about it. *Oh well, get it together,* was my thought.

I told Marshal that if we didn't start communicating that we'll be like two ships passing in the night. That statement slowly became true. I continued to give him the benefit of doubt because he was a good person. There was nothing I asked that he wouldn't do. He did the shopping. He took my clothes out the dryer after I washed them. He sat next to my bed when I was sick. This particular day I had a extremely bad headache. I literally thought I was dying. We weren't married then. But he came over when I called. I took a Motrin and laid down. When I woke up he was sitting in a chair next to my bed.

In the morning when I left for work, he'd walk me to the lobby. But what I had a problem with is him going along with whatever I said. I needed someone to take the lead sometime. He never gave his true opinion or what he really felt about anything. I guess he was hoping it would resolve itself. It didn't.

So, when I moved South in 2014, our problems still existed. I always wanted to move South. I hated the snow and cold weather in MI. Dad and I looked at houses a long time ago. He was ready to walk away from his marriage to Mom. It was a house on the same street as my favorite aunt. But Dad had a change of heart. I was a little disappointed because I had my heart set on moving. But I understood. Dad wasn't the type of person to walk away.

The only way I was able to move South was because my daughter received a job offer. She was there a year before I moved. I found an apartment online and asked her to check it out. I moved six months later with Mom and Trubbs. Marshal wasn't ready to move at that time. He had unfinished business to take care of. I continued to help him with the rent for three months. We had already talked about Mom living with us. I was not about to leave her with no one checking on her. My brothers didn't visit her often. One brothers church was walking distance to her apartment but he never stopped by to see if she needed anything. I was the one taking her grocery shopping or dropped off a meal after work. Or take her to the park, before I went home. I would also take her to church. Mom read her Bible every day until she was no longer able to read it. The days she did laundry I'd go with her to the laundry room which was located on a different floor. Marshal claimed to be okay with her living with us, but I really didn't know.

Trubbs and Baby boy helped with the move. Trubbs lived with us until Marshal was ready to move. Marshal and I spoked on the phone but it wasn't too often. He kept putting off the move. So, I said if you really didn't want to come, then don't.

Before he moved down, I'd found a church that I really enjoyed. So, I mention it to him. So, when he finally arrived, and we visited one Sunday he seemed to like it as well. Things were going well. We'd go out to dinner and talk about what improvements were needed in our marriage. A few months go by. He's becoming restless because he didn't have a job. One day we were at the mall. I noticed a security guards walking around. I suggested he put in an application for security. He was hesitate, but put in an application anyway. He got the job. Security wasn't what he wanted, but it's a job.

He wanted a job as a musician. I suggested that he speak with the organ player following Sunday service. He did and the organ player invited him to sit in on choir rehearsal. He was even asked to play a few songs. A few Sundays later he was asked to play for the choir. So, he was being considered for a position. He also met with the Pastor. However, he was so inpatient that he started looking at other churches and stop attending this particular one. I told him that he wouldn't be hired if he couldn't even attend services. He found a church that was so far out that the money he received was consumed in gas. He didn't work there long. He started complaining about not being able to find anything and how the pay wasn't as much in the South. In talking to my brother one day, I hear he wants to move back to MI. He never once said it to me, and I refused to bring it up. He always seemed unhappy. He never suggested that we do things. I eventually let him know I couldn't make him happy. He has to find happiness within himself.

Months of him moping around and complaining to my brother, I decided to speak up. So, I questioned him about it indirectly and he admitted he wanted to move back. He said things weren't the way he thought it would be. So, the following year when it was time to renew the lease on the apartment, I didn't renew it. I old him he need to make plans to move back to MI. I kindly informed him that I was looking for a two-bedroom apartment for me and Mom. He made plans and I found another apartment. I moved out a month before the lease was up. Once again, I helped with the rent. He stayed about a month and a half then moved back. His family helped with the move. Our conversation after that became less and less. The marriage could have possibly worked. However, in his mind everything was always fine. I understand him trying to avoid arguments, hoping the problem will resolve itself. However, you can't just sweep everything under the rug, thinking it will go away.

When I moved into the new apartment, I hired a housekeeper to help with laundry and light chores. Mom didn't want the housekeeper to wash her clothes or vacuum her room. Lela did her laundry and vacuumed. Approximately two weeks after moving into our new apartment Mom fell and broke her hip. She had to have hip replacement. A few days following the surgery she was then transferred to rehab. I didn't know if she would be able to return home or not. When this took place Marshal hadn't left yet. So, I talked to him to see if he'd be willing to stay. I knew I wouldn't be able to handle the rent and bills if Mom had to go to a nursing home. However, his mind was basically made up. I bid him farewell. I filed for a divorce in February of 2016.

Mom eventually returned home. She was now using a walker to get around. She was doing okay for a while. Lela took her to the park to listen to jazz music from time to time. Mom really enjoyed those times with Lela. We also took her to see her sister in Georgia. We took her to the movies or out to dinner. Mom used the walker with a seat whenever we went out. At home she used a standard walker. Although, she used her cane sometimes, she didn't use it as often as she should. She was always able to get out of bed on her own and dress herself. Lela came over to assist us both with showering. Moms' memory was good sometimes and not so good at other times. She still thought she could do things like she used to. Like when my grand babies were visiting from out of town she wanted to do things with us. One day Lela and I took my grandchildren to the pool area which was walking distance near the front office. So, we walked, well I used my scooter of course. Mom swore up and down that she can walk with us saying, "I used to go for walks all the time." Okay Mom, as you said, you used to. She got so mad with us because in her mind she still could. There were times Lela drove her down to the pool.

Mom walked around the apartment sometimes without her cane or walker and I'd have to remind her. Mom was always restless at night going to the bathroom or kitchen. I have to constantly listen out for her. She had a few falls. She fell while sitting on the edge of her bed. She fell another time in the bathroom. I called Lela to help her up every time. When she'd fall, she always thought I could help her up. She'd say, "just take my hand and help me up." No mom, I can't. We both will be on the floor. These are the times I felt so helpless and useless. At night I always kept my door partly open so I could hear her if she fell. She would close it every time when she go to the bathroom. Even after I've asked her to leave it open, she still closed it. Other than that Mom was doing okay.

This particular day in 2019, K was visiting for a few days. She was asleep in the living room. The next morning I got up to fix something to eat. I have to pass Mom's room to get to the kitchen. Mom had come out the bathroom. But she was just standing in her bedroom doorway with her walker. She asked me to help her. She said she couldn't make it any further to the bed. She said her legs felt weak. I called to K. Before K could get to the room, Mom fell. I couldn't do anything but watch her fall. K wasn't able to help her up. She was able to help her sit with her back against the ottoman. I called 911 and they took her to the hospital. K got dress and rode in the ambulance with her to the hospital.

Mom stayed in the hospital a few days before she was to return home. I spoke with the hospital social worker. told her I'm no longer able to care for Mom due to my own disability. Mom had gotten weaker, and she really didn't benefit from outpatient therapy because of her memory. I felt bad because I was not able to care for her. My nerves were on edge all the time worrying about her. I also felt bad because she wanted to come home.

Lela and I looked at different facilities and found an assisted living facility not too far from the house. Mom was sad and wanted to know when she can go home. Every time she asked that would hurt my heart a little deeper. There were days she'd be okay. She was always happy to see us. It was the leaving that was hard. Both my brothers and their families seemed to visited her more after she moved. Stubbs visited her as much as he could. Mom went into Rehab around March. By July her health was failing. It became extremely difficult for staff to bathe her. She was no longer able to get up. She wasn't eating and always in pain due to bedsores. I'm sure the staff didn't reposition her every two hours. Eventually it got to the point it hurt her to be moved. The assistant living facility director suggested hospice due to her failing health. So, we decided to put her in hospice so she could at least be comfortable. Mom passed away in August of 2019.

When Stubbs and I went to view her body at the funeral home I became angry for a split second. I was not angry with Mom or myself. I was angry because of the situation. I wanted her to wake up, but I knew she would not. I then became deeply saddened. She was not only my Mom. She was also my friend.

As a child Mom used to sing this song to wake us up. And she'd sing it until we got up.

'Get up you sleepy head, wake up.
Wake up you sleepy head get up.
It's time to rise and shine.'

Mom this prayer is for you.
God our Father,
Your power brings us to birth,
Your providence guides our lives,
And by Your command we return to dust,
Lord, those who die still live in Your presence,
Their lives change but do not end.
I pray in hope for my family,
Relatives and friends,
And for all the dead known to You alone.
In company with Christ,
Who died and now lives,
May they rejoice in Your Kingdom,
Where all our tears are wiped away.
Unite us together again in one family,
To sing Your praise forever and ever.
"Amen"

Mothers are special.
Mothers give life.
Mothers nourish you back to health when you're sick.
Mothers provide for you.
Mothers forgive you.
Mothers sacrifice for you.
Mothers help ease the pain.
Mothers love unconditionally
Mothers always have your back.
There's nothing like a mother's love.
I have to say, this is the love mom showed me. Rest in Peace mom. ♥♥

CLOSING

In closing, I want to thank you for taking the time to read my book. I hope it help you to understand me and what I've gone through and still deal with. Although things are a little more difficult than what I'm accustomed to, I'm doing pretty well. I know that I'm blessed. My four beautiful children love me, and they're blessed. I have my previous grandchildren as well. In being honest even an able-bodied person has bad days from time to time. It's only natural.

My philosophy is to enjoy the moment, enjoy the memories, enjoy the possibilities. Enjoy the things I can do and not focus on the things I can't do. I thank God for giving me strength beyond what I thought I had. I thank Him for allowing me to share my story and hopefully bless others. I'm glad to be given the opportunity to see what I can accomplish.

So please never give up on life and definitely don't give up on yourself. There is always someone worse off than you. Most of all, remember that God will not give you more than you can handle. I'm still able to drive. I moved in with my daughter a few months after Mom was admitted to rehab. Lela has three shih tzu's. I didn't like having to take over her bedroom. Unfortunately there was no other alternative. Her other two bedrooms are on the upper level. I also have my own bathroom, which is great. I no longer cook because the knobs on her stove are located in the back. I do however help with cooking Thanksgiving dinner.

I spend majority of time in my room. I will sit on the patio when the weather is nice. I will go out for appointments, hair salon, out to dinner, run errands with my daughter or visit my son. Because of COVID we don't go to the movies or the mall like we use to. My daughter and I will watch a good movie or reality shows. My daughter helps me when needed. She is truly a blessing more than she realizes. There were times I was told that I'm an inspiration to others. I hope to continue to be an inspiration. Despite all that I've gone through, I'm *still* standing.

Printed in the United States
by Baker & Taylor Publisher Services